Overcoming The Distractions (Carrots) of Life

Copyright 2024, TXU 2-424-209

Table of Contents

Table Contents..1

Introduction..2

Special Thanks... 5

What are Distractions or "Carrots" of Life? 6

Overcoming the Distraction or "Carrot" of the Unexpected....................9

Overcoming the Distraction or "Carrot" of What Seems to be Good........14

Overcoming the Distraction or "Carrot" that are Seen and Unseen.........18

Overcoming the Distraction or "Carrot" of Worry............................22

Overcoming the Distraction or "Carrot" of Denial...........................28

Overcoming the Distraction or "Carrot" of Busyness............................. 36

Overcoming the Distraction or "Carrot" of Impatience..........................41

Overcoming the Distraction or "Carrot" of Noise...........................47

Overcoming the Distraction or "Carrot" of No Accountability..................50

Overcoming the Distraction or "Carrot" of False News............................55

Overcoming the Distractions or "Carrot" of Gifts and Talents..................60

Overcoming the Distraction or "Carrot" of Miscommunication................67

Overcoming the Distractions or Carrots of Life-- Summary......................72

Round Table Discussion...73

Words Of Encouragement...74

Highlights...76

Your Challenge..77

Introduction

*The proverbial "Carrot" in this book and in my previous writing, **When Life Dangles You a Carrot**, represents the various things that distract people, every day, as we live here on earth. Distractions (Carrots of Life) keep us from focusing on the things that we have been destined to do throughout the course of our lives. The definition of distraction is to draw the sight, mind, or attention in different directions; to perplex; to confuse; as, to deter the eye; to deter the attention. In other words: Distractions are things that comes to deter one from following the right path or staying on track to accomplish their God given purpose in life.*

Distractions, both good and bad, when unaddressed, can cause us to lose focus on the key issues of life. In addition, distractions can cause us to miss out and not recognize some of the most important decisions of our life and purpose. There are "good distractions," which can occur, in our families, friendships, careers, civic & organizational commitments, various other relationships, possessions, etc.; And there are bad distractions, which occur in similar situations. Either or both can keep us so busy we can become oblivious to our surroundings, which can hinder us from making the best choices for our life and ultimately having a negative impact. It is critical that we stay focused on our purpose in this life that God has given us. If we learn how to overcome life's many distractions, this will help us to have a positive impact in our lives, family, friends, and our community.

*Please do not think that this message of overcoming distractions is an easy; one, two, three task. **It most certainly is not!** We must strive to keep moving forward each day, regardless of the distractions, detours, hinderances, etc..*

Even when setbacks occur (and they will on a regular basis), and when unplanned disasters pop up out of nowhere to knock us off course, we must equip ourselves to overcome all of these obstacles. We must learn to fight back to stay on track, or if we happen to get knocked off track: it is important to know how to get back on track, so we can overcome whatever our circumstance may be.

It will require patience, trust in God, faith, dedication, commitment to Biblical principles, time, prayer, and a circle of close friends (prayer partners), to help us stay on or to get back on track. If we happen to fall down in life after making a mistake, we must have the determination to get back up and get back on track. We do this by asking for the Lord's help to renew our thoughts every day. One of the keys to overcoming in life is reading the word of the Lord (the Bible) and allowing the truth of God's Word to lead and guide us to have faith in God, to make wise decisions in life. This is a key to overcoming obstacles in life.

In this life there are situations that cause us real Heartbreak and Pain. Occurrences such as losing a loved one, or being diagnosed with an illness, or dealing with emotional trauma. All of these occurrences can impact our focus in our day to day lives. There are times in our lives when we may feel emotional and physical pain that can make it hard to get out of bed in some mornings. There also can be times when one may need professional physical and mental therapy to help our condition. Whatever the situation/s we may have to go through, I know these are not easy things to deal with. However, we must learn that in whatever state we are in, WE CAN OVERCOME!

This book is all about, learning how to live through any situation or circumstance, trusting God each and every step of the way.

While we continue to move forward even if it is baby steps, you are still moving forward, that is all that matters. God will strengthen and empower us, through the power of His indwelling Holy Spirit, through the shed blood of Jesus Christ.

*It is for these reasons that I have written this second addition to my original book (**When Life Dangles You a Carrot**), to take us to the next level. **Overcoming Distractions (Carrots) of Life**: My goal is to provide the reader with the Biblical Principles that will Enlighten and Enable each of Us to live a most Productive and Victorious life by Overcoming the constant distractions we all face, day by day. My prayer for every reader is that you will Overcome the Distractions (Carrots) of Life: KJV: James Chapter 1 verse 4 "Let patience have her perfect work in your life, that you may be perfect, complete, in need of nothing."*

Special Thanks

To my husband Henry, thank you for all you have been to me and how you have prayed for our family and worked so hard to lead and provide for our family. You have enabled me to live a better and more fruitful life that honors God. I must say, I am a much better version of myself, because of your example, your prayers, and your God given influence on my life. Even in troubled times, I watched God, how He refines our union, so that we as a couple continue to grow stronger and closer. We have learned how to live a life together in servitude that honors the Lord Jesus Christ. **Thank You so very much and I love you.**

In memory of my mother, Margaret Davis, who left this earth in April of 2021, to be with our Lord, thank you for leaving a Godly deposit in my life. Her words to me were "Don't give up on the promises of God, for you can do all things through Christ that gives you strength day by day." (**Thank You Mom**)

Thank you, Lord Jesus, for saving me, for NOT leaving me or forsaking me through all the years and seasons of my life. There have been some seasons that I did not think I could tunnel through, BUT GOD, and his mercy he kept me through it all. I am thankful for how you call me Friend. (**Thank you Lord**)

What are The Distractions or "Carrots" of Life?

*We live in a world that is full of distractions; things that are designed to get us off track. Distractions (carrots, as I call them) deter us from the path that God has placed us here on earth to follow. Many of the distractions we face are clearly seen in our daily interaction with family, society, etc. However, there are also various unseen(spiritual) sources of constant distractions that we deal with as well. In my initial writing of "**When Life Dangles You a Carrot**" we learned that distractions can be seen as "Carrots" that are dangled before us every day. These distractions or carrots can cause our lives to go into a tailspin. It is important that we learn how to Overcome these distractions and not get on a "merry-go-round," and allow the same distractions to hinder us over-and-over again.*

The world is forever changing, and today in the 21st Century it is changing at a much faster pace than ever before. Today, changes occur so quickly, it almost seems at times that we cannot keep up with the latest changes, day after day. I believe that many of the changes in our world and in our individual lives catch people off guard and we are not aware of the impact the changes are already having on our lives.

It also appears that people in the 21st century are more desensitized to change, so when a distraction occurs in our lives, if we do not recognize the impact it has immediately upon our lives! In some cases, we do not recognize the impact until it is too late to make a meaningful change.

Every day there is something new happening, something new is discovered, something new is developed, something new is planned. While many of these "new things" can be helpful (technology, etc.,), on the other hand, many of these new discoveries DISTRACT us from focusing on what we should and must do day by day.

Modern technologies should not supersede current responsibilities, which often happens when a new and better way distracts people from taking care of their current responsibilities.

*All the "New Things" can be a major distraction to our current responsibilities. Did you hear what I said, Not every week, Not every month, BUT **EVERYDAY;** There is something happening in the world, in our country, in our state, in our community, in our home, etc. where something or someone is endeavoring to DISTRACT US FROM DOING THE RIGHT THINGS, OR HANDLING OUR RESPONSIBILITIES WITH OUR FAMILIES, JOBS, COMMUNITY ORGANIZATIONS, CHURCH, ETC., TO MAINTAIN AND TO ACCOMPLISH OUR GOD GIVEN PURPOSE.*

If you do not believe me, simply turn on the morning news or the evening news broadcast or look on your cell phone or other devices: something new is being reported continually. The news is reported to make us aware of what is happening in our city, state, country, and the world at large. However, most of the Daily News we hear or see, via Social Media, Television, Radio, Word of Mouth; each day, ends up distracting us from focusing on our day to day most important goals and responsibilities in life.

Now, I understand why my mother use to sing the old hymn: "One day at a time, Sweet Jesus, that's all I'm asking from You." That old hymn suggests that we need to be thankful to God Almighty for each day; and learn how to focus on today, one day at a time; and not be distracted by what happened yesterday or what may happen tomorrow.

To be able to stay in character, to stay focused on what you have planned for TODAY, and to learn how to maintain your faith in God; when you can remain undistracted by what is going on around you; that is a day of **Victory!**

Psalms: chapter 16 verse 11 states, You will show me the path of life. I have come to understand that there is a specific path that we all need to be journeying on in order to experience life while travelling through this land. Realizing this is not our permanent home.

In the meantime, there is purpose and meaning while we are here. God has chosen us as instruments to help a dying generation to know the truth. Right now, the time we are living in seems to be dark and chaotic which can be difficult to say focused on the right things that are God design. That is why the attacks, obstacles and confusion is always larking around in order to deter us from staying on the path of Life.

My goal in this writing is to bring awareness to what is going on in and around our circumstances, workplaces, families, health, finances, and our mental mind sets and most of all our spiritual growth in God. Practicing every day to focus or regain our focus is so powerful to keep moving forward. We just need to be aware when something comes up as a distraction not to get stuck.

Hopefully, this writing will provide the reader with a clear understanding of "the things that can so easily set us back (Hebrews 12:1)," the things that get us off track from accomplishing our God given purpose.

My prayer for every reader is that this will be the year that WE overcome all the distractions that have held us back, and those distractions that we will face in the days to come. Let this be the year that we move up to a higher way of thinking and living, and that we live as OVERCOMERS who lives above the Distractions (Carrots) of this life!

Overcoming the Distraction (Carrot) of the Unexpected

News flash; as I began to draft this book I ran "smack dab" into Mr.(D), Mr. Distraction. Ok; this was the perfect moment for me to practice what I am about to preach. I received a disturbing phone call that was unexpected. Yes, it was one of those calls where there was nothing I could do to calm down a friend who was experiencing a meltdown. After receiving the phone call, I turned my computer off. I endeavored to listen, and I prayed to help my friend. However, my concentration on what I was doing had been broken. It was then that I realized the fact that the unexpected call had totally distracted me from what I was doing. After the call, I put my coat on and went for a walk. I called my brother to talk and pray with him about the friend I had just talked with. We both came to the same conclusion. Just keep on praying. Afterward, while praying and talking to the Lord, I decided I am going to praise Him (God), despite confusion and situation with my friend. I decided that I was going to praise God, despite being upset.

One lesson I learned from this experience and from my life in general is the fact that: You have the power to change the way you think by changing your perspective, changing your environment, or changing the way you are handling the situation. It is a matter of deciding what you will do to change your perspective. Many people choose to ruminate on their problems and do not attempt to seek God or other trusted confidantes to help them for relief, counsel, encouragement, or enlightenment in situations that are unexpected. Others choose to "stay stuck" in their old ways of doing things, which causes them to stay in the same rut, not moving forward and learn how to Overcome the unexpected. The battleground we face, day by day, is in our mind or our day-to-day affairs. This can be a real struggle; that is why we need to ask for Gods' help in times and situations that are unexpected.

I have always resorted to the Bible for direction in situations like this. I go to the Book of Psalms because King David sought God in situations where he experienced unexpected occurrences. Many of the Psalms were written by King David, to provide with "God's Peace and Direction" in times when he faced unexpected and troubling experiences. I have read Psalms: 42 and verse 6 where King David was going through a very rough and emotional time. Despite the emotional stress he was dealing with at that time, he concluded: I will yet praise the Lord! He had a yet praise!!! It is important in these times to consider "the way we think must be stronger than our feelings." This is how we Overcome the heavy emotions, by not allowing these emotions to weigh us down.

Emotions can be so strong that they have the power to deter us from making good sound decisions and prevent us from continuing on the right path. Thank God, he gave us emotions, they serve a good purpose so that we have feelings that go with various situations. Emotions also are a good sign that we are still alive and can feel the impact of what we are going through or dealing with. In addition, emotions provide us with feelings that allow us to adjust, choosing to not blow up. However, there are times in our lives, if we want to overcome obstacles that are getting us down, we can and must choose to take control of our feelings and exercise self-control, patience, and peace.

If we do like King David did in the Psalms, Praise is what we do at times when we do not know what to do, but we must take control of our feelings. Praise invites God presence into our lives and situations. Praise to God will also take our minds off of our problems, allowing us to overcome our difficult circumstances. Praise to God also will allow us to focus on the One (God) who is truly in control of everything; knowing that He will lead and guide us to the correct solution to our problems with renewed thoughts. Whatever you are facing right this moment, Praise to God will calm your mind and spirit to help you in your time of need.

Go ahead right now: Give God thanks; Thank Him for who He is (Jehovah Jirah-He is our Provider). Go ahead and Praise God for a few seconds, see what happens. God is the lifter of our soul. If you learn to do this in the times when you feel down or all alone, you will find yourself coming back to life, rising up and getting your thoughts and life together, combing your hair, washing your face, and refocusing for the day.

I have also noticed, when I started Praising, Acknowledging and Thanking God for His presence and His amazing impact on my life: I have learned how to cast all my cares on Him: Then I started to realize that the unexpected distractions stopped being the focus for me at that time. There was a time when I would let the unexpected distraction get me off track for days at a time. This would keep me from being focused on the right things to keep moving forward.

I was distracted in several ways when I decided to author this book. As soon as I was able to identify the fact that things that were happening in my life were distractions to keep me from writing and completing this book, I was able to quickly break free from the unexpected distraction. I had to decide on whether I would stay stuck and be distracted, or if I would be free and keep moving forward. It was important for me to get this message out concerning distractions and that is what kept me pushing forward to get this book completed.

Our thoughts are our reality, or they will become your reality. When we experience distractions, we must allow our thoughts to override our emotions to enable us to broaden our perspective and see things in a new and better way. This must be a daily practice, a practice of renewing your thoughts and reminding yourself to think deeply or meditate on our goals and the right things before reacting. This has to be a daily practice. This practice will enable us to overcome obstacles and achieve our goals.

After my walk, I started to shift my thoughts onto a higher level of thinking; and to elevate my mind on things that are above the problem that sought to hinder and prevent me from focusing on my goals. When I focused my thoughts on the Word of God, the Creator of heaven and earth, the almighty God that can do anything but fail, the one who is a present help in the time of trouble; **The Case is Close***d! I will overcome my problem! This experience helped me learn how to refocus and how to calm myself down and get back to finishing what I had begun.*

So, how do we overcome <u>Unexpected</u> distractions? (Good Question?) First, we must admit that there are many things that happen to us that seem to be routine or regular occurrences, which are actually things that come to blindside and are truly Distractions. After we admit that many routine happenings in our lives are actually distractions, it will take some effort and pushing back, and I mean PUSH BACK, to recognize and effectively overcome in these areas of life!

An unexpected distraction will make you feel disoriented, confused, and sometimes discouraged, because it is not what you expected. This is when we must learn to push back and replace a bad thought with a good thought or a promise from God's Word. We must exchange bad thoughts with what God has said in his Word and trust him for what he has spoken through His Word. Do you trust him? Do you trust what the Bible says?

Trusting in God will keep us sound in our thinking and prevent us from running away from situations that are obstacles to distract us from our daily goals. I have come to understand more the Bible, passage in Matthew chapter: 6 verse 11. It states: "Lord gives us our daily bread." Another interpretation says: "Lord give us what we need today to sustain us through the tests we will endure today." In those unexpected situations, we must learn to Listen! As we listen we will also learn to trust God. Listening and Trusting God are not options, They are a **Must***!!*

We must be fervent in prayer, and we must acknowledge God, learn to give Him praise: this practice will truly enable us to overcome any distraction. We must push back, and I emphasize, "push back," the negative thoughts by prayer & praise in our daily worship of almighty God. This practice is how we should engage and build our relationship with God. This practice will enable us to Overcome many distractions, especially the Unexpected Distractions. Our weapon to overcome the unexpected distractions is Prayer and Praise to God, we must practice this on a regular basis.

*This will raise our antenna to be on high alert for our adversary, the devil, who as a roaring lion, walketh about, seeking whom he may devour, 1Peter: chapter 5 verse 8. I am persuaded that if we follow the Lord God Almighty, The Prince of Peace, and if we seek his direction and example, we will have the **Peace of God** despite the adversary.*

We will overcome any and every distraction in life that comes to get us off course. Some of us may overcome immediately some of us it may take time but never-the-less we will, we shall Overcome. Because of Gods strength not our own but his strength is what causes us to be Overcomers!!!

Thought Questions for the Carrot of the Unexpected

What is the first thing we should do when the unexpected shows up?

Do you hold onto a distraction longer than you should?

Overcoming the Distraction (Carrot) of What Seems to be good.

*Most of us have heard the saying "everything that glitters is not gold." There are many things in life that appear to be good, but the true value is not realized until you get close to it. You must observe the object to get the details. Then you must find out what you are dealing with that has been dangled before you. Life in general presents us with many situations that "seem to be good." Situations like; a Job that offers more money: a man or a woman that appears to be a good person to marry and spend the rest of your life with, positive recognition for something you have done etc. While all of these situations, on the surface "seem to be good," the Bible teaches us and life in general teaches us: though things may "seem" to be right, the conclusion could be destructive if you do not dig a little deeper to get a clear understanding of what you are dealing with. As stated in <u>Proverbs 14:12</u>, <u>there is a way that **seems** right to a man, but its end is the way of death.</u>*

In many of our life experiences, everything that glitters in not gold, and things that appear to be good do not always mean that they are the right thing for us to do. In addition, some things may appear to be good, perhaps the timing (right now vs. later) is wrong. You may need time to grow, mature, and develop so you do not fail prematurely. So, what seems to be good for now, the timing may not be good. (As opposed to five years from now when you are equipped and ready to handle the situation).

Things that happen in our lives that seem to be good for us can give us a false impression of improving our current conditions. This readily can happen when we allow pride and self-promotion into our hearts and minds, based on the things that happen to us that "Seem" to be good. Pride leads to destruction (Proverbs 16:18). Pride does this by producing arrogance and selfishness, thinking that we have the power to do good and accomplish these things on our own ability.

Every good and perfect gift comes from above (God Almighty). In Him we live, move, and have our very being. Therefore, we should always realize where our help and strength comes from.

We must always recognize God first, in every Good situation of our lives. If we do not, pride will enter in, and when it does it always has an unfruitful and negative ending. Once again, when pride enters our thoughts, the unseen warfare begins, and pride never has a good ending.

*This is when we must look to God for direction and stay focused on his Word no matter how tempting a carrot may dangle in front of us. We must Watch as well as Pray: Mark chapter :14 verse 38. Yes, we must watch and be alert. Do you have your spiritual eyes open? God will lead us on the right path and not just what **"seems"** to be the good path, but rather the path that leads to Life.*

*Fellow readers, there is a way to avoid what **"seems"** to be good and keep moving forward, doing the Will of God. Always ask yourself this question when these seemingly good carrots are dangle before us: What I am committing to will it please God? Our dependency must be fully on the Lord Jesus Christ, recognizing Jesus as our Savior, the Holy Spirit of God as our Keeper, God as our Father, and give no credit to our flesh and the systems of this world. God Almighty deserves ALL the Glory, ALL the time.*

If there are unexpected or expected blessings that happens in our life, God deserves the Glory, because every good and perfect gift comes from above (James 1:17). Things will occur in our daily lives, some appear to be good, some appear to be bad. Pray and God will give us confidence in our spirit and stability in our thoughts to know what to do in every situation. **God Is Good!!!!**

Thought Questions for the Carrot of what Seems to be Good

What does better vs. best mean to you?

Have you ever been tempted to chase after what appeared to be good But yet not the best thing over all?

Notes (Your thoughts)

Overcoming the Distractions (Carrot) that are Seen and Unseen

We must recognize the fact that, regardless of our status, name, rank, background, finances, history, nationality, etc. Distractions will continue to occur in our daily lives. DISTRACTIONS WILL HAPPEN: TO ALL PEOPLE, ALL RACES, ALL CREEDS, ALL COLORS, ALL NATIONALITIES, ALL NATIONS, ALL COUNTRIES!!!

To overcome distractions, we must first recognize that they are real, and they are inevitable! We cannot avoid them, We cannot get rid of them; However, we can OVERCOME THEM IF WE TAKE THE TIME TO LEARN HOW TO LIVE WITH THEM AND EMPLOY THE BIBLICAL PRINCIPLES THAT WILL ENABLE US TO OVERCOME DISTRACTIONS EVERY TIME THEY SHOW UP!!!!!

Every Single Day, Like it or not, come hell or high water, rich, or poor, Black, or White, Christian or Atheist, Democrat or Republican; Distractions will come into our lives! Distractions are real, they are alive, and they are at work, moving in our space, crowding our atmosphere, impacting our lives, and in many cases, negatively! Distractions are caused by things going on around us, things in our city, our state, our country, and the World at Large.

These "Things" that manifest themselves as "Distractions" are things that affect our lives in both the; **"Seen and Unseen"** *Realms. What does this mean, in the "seen and unseen realms?"*

The things, or happenings, or forces in our lives that are **"Seen Distractions,"** *are easy to detect. For example, You get up in the morning and you are rushing to get ready, and you are in a hurry to get to work. Then, you back your car out of your driveway, on your way to work. However, you fail to look in the rear-view mirror as you back out, and you back into a fence that is behind you. The fence was visible, but you failed to look in the rear-view mirror, so you hit the fence. This is a* **"Seen Distraction."**

You could have easily avoided the accident by simply looking into your rear-view mirror and stopping prior to hitting the fence.

*On the other hand, **"Unseen Distractions or Unseen Forces"** can cause distractions as well. These are things you **"Cannot see with the naked eye,"** however, they can cause severe damage to your quality of life, your future, and your purpose here on earth. Now you may be a person who does not believe in the Unseen Realm, and that is understandable. There are many that do not believe in the unseen realm. However, the reality in the world we live in suggests that there is an **"Unseen Realm"** that is just as real as the **"Seen Realm."** Day-to-day living here on earth reveals the truth and the impact that the **"Unseen Realm"** has on our day to day lives. When you consider **"Unseen Distractions"** and the significant impact they have on our lives, consider these examples:*

1. <u>**The Unseen WIND of the weather**</u>: *The wind blows in the air and has a major impact on our weather and living conditions. It also is a major factor in the weather distractions and destruction in our day-to-day lives, such as storms, hurricanes, tornadoes, etc. We cannot visually see the wind with the naked eye. We cannot see hurricanes or tornado winds or storms, and where they come from; or where they may end up. However, you can clearly see the impact and the devastation it causes as it blows and moves across the land and seas.* **Unseen Distractions operate in the exact same fashion**; *You cannot visually see the wind itself or where the power of the wind is coming from, however, you can easily see the physical impact as the wind moves everything in its pathway, and in some cases, causes mass destruction to our land and sea, or how severe weather can impact everyone in its pathway. We never see the actual wind itself as it moves in numerous ways and places, However, we see its impact, whether it is cold chills up our spine, or fallen trees in its destructive pathway.*

2. **<u>The Unseen Viruses and Diseases in the Air</u>:** *Starting in the year 2020, the entire world was distracted for over two years, and still is reeling from the impact of an **Unseen virus** named Covid-19. You cannot visually see the virus with the naked eye, but its effect is felt worldwide with millions of deaths attributed to its' "Unseen viral effects." This is another instance of "**Unseen**" distractions that can have a significant effect on our lives. If the virus could be seen with the naked eye, it would be simple for us to devise ways to get rid of it or take other actions to prevent its negative impact. However, the virus operates in the "Unseen realm," so we must produce ways to constantly fight and protect against its negative impacts, such as vaccines,' masks, frequent hand washing, social distancing, etc. These are ways we have learned to Overcome the negative impacts of COVID-19. This is the same way we can learn to overcome other "Unseen Distractions (carrots), which constantly seek to interrupt our day-to-day living. We must put into practice the preventative measures, tools, behaviors, which will protect us from our Unseen enemies.*

We cannot deny the realities of the Wind of the weather or the COVID-19 Viruses. We have to acknowledge that there are unseen realities such as the COVID-19 virus and the wind of the weather (hurricanes and tornadoes). We may not think much about these Unseen Distractions, but the fact of this matter is that "Unseen distractions" are real.

Until we face up to this fact and put into practice the tools that can enable us to Overcome the Unseen Distraction, we can become stuck and off track. If we do not recognize the fact that unseen distractions are real, we will be wasting a lot of time and energy trying to make sense of what we cannot see. Just because we cannot see a disturbance or chaos happing we cannot deny that it is real.

We must prepare for these distractions and learn how to overcome them. First of all, God is not a God of confusion. When you are around a lot of confusion something is going on in the unseen that will manifest confusion, discord, division, etc...

Seen and Unseen Distractions are designed to force us to get off track and to become unfocused on the things that are most important. For instance: Note the following list of impacts that the Unseen Power of Distraction had during the COVID-19 pandemic, beginning in 2020 and continuing up to today:

1. *Divorce Rate: Increased*
2. *Inflation: Increased*
3. *Mental Illness: Increased*
4. *Suicide Rate: Increased*
5. *Violence & Murder rate: Increased*

When we consider the negative impact of these statistics, on our families, our communities, our country as a whole and the world at large, it is extremely important for us to Stay Focused and not be distracted from the people and things that are most important to us. In the Bible, we are instructed by the words of Jesus to pursue the Lord's ways first (Matthew 6:33); and if we seek The Lord first and His Righteousness and His Kingdom; everything that we need to live and serve here on this earth will be given to us.

When growing up as a young child in church, we had what was called testimonial service. This was a time during worship when we would get up, one at a time, and we would say "I thank God for protecting me from dangers, seen and unseen." ***I UNDERSTAND EXACTLY WHAT THEY MEANT BY THE "SEEN AND THE UNSEEN" NOW!***

Overcoming the Distraction (Carrot) of Worry

The following are some examples of what the distractions of worry can look like and how they can negatively impact your thoughts and your life in general. You are confronted with an unexpected crisis: "Your child is on the wrong path of life; You are laid off from your job without any advance notice, etc.; You are diagnosed with a sickness or disease with no prior symptoms or issues; Your email or electronic account gets hacked, etc.. These unexpected and upsetting situations happen to us all. However, in some of these situations, when we do not have any immediate solutions they are the cause of additional stress and constant worry.

Sometimes our immediate outward response is the Big Façade: "Oh I am fine, I am good, I will be okay." However, the truth of the situation is that on the inside and in our mind we are starting to worry obsessively because we do not know what to do! In the meantime, we can fail to realize things we start doing, subconsciously, that you can start turning to for temporary relief due to the stress and worry. You realized after you have eaten not one, but two sandwiches, a huge bowl of ice cream with whip cream and chocolate sauce over it! As you sit and think(worry) about your problem, you continue to eat, profusely, without being aware of how much you are eating, with all kinds of thoughts going on in your mind; worrying and not knowing what to do or how you should feel. You think that all the food you are eating is helping you cope with the problem you face. However, you fail to realize that food is never a coping mechanism when the problem is in the mind.

Worry is a mental and/or spiritual issue and food is never the solution. Worry primarily occurs when we have a problem that needs to be solved and we do not know what to do or how to deal with it. This can be a huge distraction because there will always be things that we will face in our day-to-day lives that we have not dealt with before or things that we do not know how to manage. This is why God has provided us with help, through His presence in our lives, through His Words, through family and friends, through information and education. However, we must accept God's help from all of these sources because worrying can be detrimental to our health and well-being.

Whenever worry arises in our lives or situations, we should always be aware that there is help available. Trouble will arise, storms will rage, but there is always help somewhere close by, when God is in our lives. Some people may cringe at the thought of trusting an unseen God to help us overcome our worries. However, with the problems we face day to day, trusting in God to overcome worry is just as real as trusting a friend or relative.

You may not be able to see him, but you know he is the GOD that is there, because you tried him before and what happen, he brought you out! You may be experiencing a tug of war that is raging in your mind, and you eat food to camouflage it: That is the distraction of worry. It can also manifest itself when you are trying to figure something out and you pace the floor, back and forth, late into the night. What is that? That is the distraction of worry! Will pacing back and forth help me think more clearly or think of a solution? Maybe it will, or maybe it will not. However, you will continue to Worry as you are pacing back and forth, still causing frustration until you produce, what you think is a solution.

To Overcome this spirit of worry, the question we should be asking ourselves is: What can I do to bring comfort and bring peace of mind so I can best manage this situation?

Is there a way I can free myself from this worry and constant concern over the decision I need to make or what I need to do? Is there a way I can rid myself of this worry and frustration, so I can overcome these thoughts and move forward with my life?

It is time to move forward, time to go forth. For some we have worn ourselves out we have to get out of the distraction of worrying and live more peacefully.

Yes, you can overcome the distraction of worry. However, you do need to put your trust in someone who is truly bigger than you and I. Matthew 11:29-30 "take my yoke (tie yourself up to the Lord), learn from me, for my yoke is easy and my burden is light, saith the Lord. The fact that the carrot of Worry has dangled so often before us we have been distracted by its powerful forces; Jesus is saying, connect with me and my words, and you will find rest from your worries and fears, and I will ease your mind.

Today in the 21st century, worry is one of the key contributors to our mental health crisis, causing sleepless nights, constant worries and for millions, no peace of mind. Food, drugs, alcohol, and many other things are used as coping mechanisms, to this day, have not provided a permanent and stable solution to the **distractions of worry.**

To overcome the distractions of worry, we unquestionably need the help of the Lord God Almighty, His Word and His Holy Spirit. In addition, and especially important, we must obediently submit to God's Words (Holy Bible), which leads to Peace of Mind and overcoming in our day to day lives. Jesus gave the key in Matthew 11:28 (Come unto ME all who labor and are heavy laden, and I will give you rest).

Praying, long relaxing walks, and meditating on God's Word will enable us to stand on God's promises and encourage us to keep us moving forward. Talking to a close friend who is a good listener, who knows how to listen, who knows God and will pray with you, will also help. In addition, Jesus also mentioned in Matthew 17:21 States (However, this kind does not go out except by prayer and fasting) sometimes we have to turn our plate down and go to God for deliverance in certain areas. It may be for you, your family, or the world at large to unload the burden we are carrying.

Fasting and prayer coupled together, we must practice regularly so we can grow, control any worries, and learn to trust God. When life becomes stressful and challenging, and circumstances really hit us hard we must not let worrying become our best friend. However, we must learn to rely on God and trust him, trust his Word, and learn to rest in him completely. We must learn to trust in the fact that God is our launching pad and our landing place. If he brought us out before he could do it again. Let us trust and obey God's Words, while allowing His instructions to lead us into a quiet place within.

Luke: 21:33 States (Heaven and earth will pass away, but My words will by no means pass away). We can trust God's Word (the Bible), for guidance in all of our concerns, temptations, and trials. We can have confidence in God's Word and not trust in our own solutions. We must learn to trust in His guidance, and instructions, knowing that God's guidance has stood the test of time, and it can and will do the same for us if we trust Him.

To consistently overcome our problems and worries we must also learn to praise God instead of worrying. <u>It is impossible to praise God and worry at the same time. Try it and see!</u> If you are worrying about anything right now, stop what you are doing and start praising God for his goodness and His mercy towards us. I am sure you will soon have no other choice but to turn those worries into praise!

*Thank God because He knows all and sees all. Thank God because He is a promise keeper and a miracle worker. Thank God because He cares for us. He is the only one that can take our issues and worries from life's circumstances and give us peace. So go ahead; Thank Him, Praise Him, and cast all of your cares over to our great God and Promise keeper, the Lord Jesus Christ (**<u>He is a mighty good Catcher</u>**)!*

Thought Questions concerning the Distractions of Worry:

Are you a worrier?

What are some things you could do to not worry?

Have you ever tried to "Praise the Lord" while worries were on your mind?

Overcoming the Distractions (Carrots) of Denial

*Denial is one of those conditions that can go unaddressed because we refuse to admit it exists. To some, denial takes the form of a safe hiding place as you endeavor to deal with day-to-day problems that are not being dealt with. Denial develops from various circumstances in life. At times denial arises from the pains and disappointments of our past. Denial can also develop when guilt or unforgiveness lingers within you. Only you know if you are truly hiding and/or protecting yourself from pain; and when you refused to deal with it, you are clearly in **Denial.***

Life can bring us to a point where we do not want to see things as they really are. However, at the same time, even though we refuse to acknowledge things as they really are, if we deny the fact that they exist, we will eventually have a bigger issue when the situation we have been denying "snowballs" into a huge iceberg that stops us from moving forward in life. This is what Denial can lead to! You now have a much larger obstacle that will be more difficult to deal with. All because, Denial kept you from addressing the problem head on.

Recently, I had my yearly eye examination. My vision was slightly worse than the previous year. I found an eye glass store where I could get my new glasses, which had been prescribed for me by my eye doctor. The store was having a special "BOGO sale," buy one, get a second pair of glasses free! I jumped on this BOGO promotion and purchased my glasses, with the second pair for free! After the purchase, I noticed, while wearing my original prescribed glasses, something was wrong with the lenses. I looked in the mirror and my new glasses gave me an unusual look that I did not like. What I saw in the mirror looked distorted. I called the eyeglass store to question them on the materials used to make my new glasses.

*The technician explained to me that they were made from extremely superior quality materials that were "top of the line (obviously, a new material that was different than what I was used to)." I was not convinced that this new material was of superior quality because I could not see as clearly as I previously could with my old glasses. What I did not realize was the fact that my new glasses corrected my **current vision**.*

Over the previous two years, my eyesight had deteriorated somewhat (which I had not realized). What I was now seeing was what I actually looked like, and what things truly looked like with new glasses that gave me 20/20 vision two years later!

*In life there are times when you will only see yourself clearly when you "renew your vision" and get your glasses updated to see how things really look in the present day. There comes a time when we have to renew our focus with a current set of lenses, leaving the past vision behind; Putting on a new and current set of lenses in life, accepting the **current situation** that is in front of us. My current vision was blurred when I used my old glasses. I could not see what was really in front of me. Actually, I was denying what was right in front of me. Over those past two years, my vision had deteriorated slightly. I needed new lenses to adjust my vision to see clearly in the present moment. When I got my new glasses the mirror was showing me all the delicate details on my face and the new glasses magnified my facial details and caused me to take a deeper look at myself (I was aging!!!). I needed the new glasses to stop denying what was really right in front of me; the fact that I was getting older, which I could clearly see with the new glasses on!*

Have you ever stopped to examine yourself through the most current window of your eyes? If so, what story will you see? Have you looked at yourself with the intent of leaving the past behind and moving on to what is currently in front of you? Have you become comfortable at pretending that things are okay? Knowing deep down inside you must deal with those buried truths that you do not want to revisit. Have you failed to recognize the truth of your pain, and made wrong choices that have blurred your vision, and caused you to deny the truth?

*If we are to overcome major obstacles in our lives, there does come a time when we must stop **Denying** the truth. We must stop disregarding what is immediately in front of us, refusing to see the reality of our situations that are currently at hand. We must stop refusing to recognize the monsters of our past that continue to show up in our rear-view mirror and cause us to veer off the good path that we are on. More importantly, if we are to overcome the distractions of denial, we must regularly check up on our vision of our day-to-day lives and look with the **current vision** from a Godly perspective.*

If we do not periodically examine ourselves, we will deny that certain issues exist in our lives, and we will be held back from growing into the person that God has destined us to be. We can easily deny our true needs, and never overcome critical obstacles in our lives. We will hinder our personal and spiritual growth because we are denying the critical areas in our lives that need to be addressed. When we deny and overlook these critical areas in our lives, we will deny ourselves to become overcomers. If we are not careful, denial can lead to destructive behaviors and relationships etc...

Let us be wise and learn how to overcome the distractions of denial by examining ourselves regularly. Making sure we can see our way clearly and making sure we are doing those things that keep us in the will of God and in good standing with our friends and loved ones. Yes, it may hurt, and it may seem as though you are never going to understand some things, because not everything is going to make sense. However, you must continue to push forward, being honest with yourself and with others. Do not try to deny or deflect the truth. Deal with the issues as they arise. If we follow this path, we will always expose the dark areas of our lives with the light of God's word. God's word also shines light into our situations. Denial can be a form of darkness as it seeks to hide the light of a situation. However, light always exposes darkness, which means the darkness will disappear when the light appears. Overcoming the darkness of denial with the truth and the light will always show us the right way that we must take. (I am a witness to the light).

Denial can also cause us to be irresponsible and cause us to shun responsibility due to mistakes and/or wrong choices that we have made in life. Some decisions we make in life, especially at a youthful age, have lifelong impacts. We must always remember, there are no problems, where God cannot solve them. We can still overcome, if we put our faith and trust in God and what He has instructed us to do in His word (the Bible). Denial will only cause us to live in the pain of a problem for a much longer period than we need to. We must face the truth about what we have been denying and allow the truth of God's words to sink deep down into our heart and soul. Let it sink down to the degree that we want to do whatever God says. This will allow God, by His Holy Spirit, to work in our lives.

Overcoming the spirit of denial can happen to you anywhere when you allow the Spirit of God to work in your life. Most people think the Spirit of God just works in your life while you are in church or some type of religious gathering. However, to overcome the spirit of denial you can be anywhere: You may be in the store, or you can be walking in your neighborhood, and you see someone, or you hear something said that triggers something inside of you that you thought was dead. At that moment, all of a sudden, your emotions brings down tears from your eyes, like a flood gate opening. Whatever caused the tears to trigger, they came to wash away the weights that you may have been carrying for a long time. Emotional situations like this can catch you anywhere, when you are driving your car, while you are in the middle of laughing about something, then the next moment you realize, the tears start flowing. I sense a washing and renewal for someone right now as you are reading this book as it ministers to you, let him wash away the sting of the past.

My prayer is: Lord wash us from our past memories that try to hold us captive, our past mistakes, cleanse us in your sacrificial blood, so that we can become clean from our sins, clean from our past, cleanse us and make us whiter the snow. (Amen somebody).

This will bring us to a place where we will have to do challenging work. The challenging work may involve letting go of past issues and emptying yourself from the current baggage that you may have been hiding behind. Unloading and letting go of Shame, quilt, trauma, and failures etc..

These issues may be hard to address at times because you may have had no control over what occurred. However, you still must deal with these issues, because denying their existence will only deepen the problem. You were not designed to carry so much weight. There is One that is strong and mighty that can bear the load his name is Jesus Christ!

What is your story you have been Denying? What is that hidden thing in your life that needs to be dealt with? What circumstance have you been looking at with "old lenses" and have not been able to see clearly? It is time to put on those new corrective lenses. Whatever the Denial is that has been holding you back, we must run ahead of the issues. We are overdue for a new perspective on life. When we can get to a place to see deeper and not just on the surface of things, we can begin to focus on the right things. We must tell ourselves; I will LIVE and not Die. For the distraction of denial will not hold me captive any longer.

The truth from the Word of God will speak to the Denial and begin the healing process. 1Corinthians 13:12 states: For now, we see through a glass, darkly; but then face to face: now I know in part; but then shall I know even as I am known.

Let this year be your year to totally break free and embrace the healing power of God's word into your heart (open your eyes and see.) Freedom comes from facing the things that have held you captive for some time. The good news is, you do not have to do it alone, Jesus is there for you every step of the way. Psalms 34:18 The Lord is nigh unto them that are of a broken heart; he saves those crushed in spirit. This all depends on how do you see Christ? Is he a big God or is he small in your eyes? The more you get to know him for the Great God he is the better you can trust him, because he knows our secret place.

Repeat after me, I am An Overcomer, say it again, I am an Overcomer!!!!!

Thought Questions for the Carrot of Denial

Are you hiding behind Guilt, Shame, or past trauma?

What are some ways we wear different masks to cover up?

Notes (What is Your Story?)

Overcoming the Distraction (Carrot) of Busyness

Today in the 21st Century we, as a people and in every society, are busier than ever before in history. With all the modern technology, social media, "instant everything," at our fingertips; instead of making our lives easier, life on earth just gets busier and busier! We are constantly trying to get things done faster, complete our tasks sooner, endeavoring to be more efficient, we end up being busy, and more busy! This leads to more stress, which leads to distress, which leads to more unrest, which negatively impacts our mental health and ultimately causes many of our lives, families, business, etc., to become a big mess!!.

Why are we so busy? Are we busy because we are bored? Are we busy because we have nothing else to do? Are we busy chasing a dream? Are we busy trying to keep up with the Jones? Many of us are busy as ever and not accomplishing the things that God put us on this earth to do. Many of us are busy like the energizer bunny where his battery seemingly never runs out. However, as we keep it moving like the Energizer Bunny, eventually our battery will go dead! More people need to hear and know that busyness does not always mean you are accomplishing your God given purpose. When one continues on this busy path we could veer off on another path that is not designed for us.

In the beginning of time, the Bible states that God created the Heavens, the Earth, Animals, and lastly, Mankind (Genesis 1-2). The Bible mentions how God rested on the seventh day, and this was all considered to be something that is "Good."

This example is one good reason we all need to take some regular rest from our busy life schedules each week and prepare for the next week of life and adventure. The busyness of day-to-day life takes a great toll on our mind, our body, and our spirit. If we do not take some time out to rest and regroup, allowing our bodies to repair and renew, we can easily exhaust our mind, body, and spirit. This is quite common in our fast paced 21st Century lifestyles and it is what I refer to as the Distraction or **Carrot of Busyness.**

We live in a time when it is important to be active and involved in the necessities of life in the 21st Century. In the United States and in most of the places in the world, it is necessary to work, make some type of living, care for family, loved ones, provide for yourself and others, food, clothing, and shelter, etc. We have daily commitments, chores, necessities, family, and for some, being a care giver for our elderly parents, etc.

However, even though we are living busy lives, it is essential that we take time out each week to get rest, to reflect on the things that are important, and to consider needed adjustments each week so we can remain healthy, in mind, body, and spirit. In addition, we must take time out each week to reflect on our day-to-day relationships with others, so we can remain effective in our day-to-day business, social, and community relationships. Once you recognize that you are getting too busy it is good that you take some time to reevaluate your daily life and schedule.

How do we do this? One good practice is to start your daily life with prayer to the most high God and meditation. We must learn that God is our source to meet all our needs. If we can learn to daily pray, breathe a prayer to God just as you take a deep breath each morning. Relax and just talk to God. Tell God all about your struggles, concerns, issues, schedule, etc..

The Bible says, "the steps of a good man are ordered by the Lord" (Psalms 37: 23). So, if we can learn to pray daily and tell God about our struggles, He will order our steps and bring organization into our lives. With a more organized life comes a clear understanding to know exactly what you should be focused on and what you need to leave alone.

Therefore, learn to relax each morning as you turn your day over to God from the very beginning. When we take time out each morning to slow down and give our schedules and our concerns over to God, we give God an opportunity to come into our lives every day. We will soon learn that God's presence, His Spirit, will come into our daily lives and Help us evaluate what adjustments need to be made each day. We may just need to have some physical rest. Taking time out each day to self-evaluate and rest gives us the opportunity to evaluate if any adjustments need to be made. This type of daily evaluation is good because it enables us to set our priorities for the day and not become busy about the wrong things.

*The **Distraction of busyness** can affect not only us as individuals, but it can have an impact on our children, other family members, friends, co-workers, etc.. There is a common tendency for a person that is too busy to become more likely to be irritable and more easily agitated. You formerly at one time liked your family and neighbors and friends, now it has become a burden to call and check on them. When you are too busy mentally, emotionally, and spiritually you cannot show up fully if you wanted to. When is the last time you took a break from busyness, took a vacation, or had some leisure time to unwind and laugh and play. I know for some of us that is so foreign because it has been so long.*

That is why it is important to establish time each day to pray and meditate so we can get focused on the right things at the start of our day and learn how to have a more balanced life. This will enable us to not be distracted by everything that keeps coming our way.

When we are mentally tired, our thinking is not as sharp as it should be. This can lead to making so many mistakes. It is time to be refreshed and renewed. When I use the word renewed it means to re-new do something new and different to get a better outcome then ending up worn out.

We must involve God in every fine detail of our life and ask for his Wisdom. We must stop confusing the busyness for thinking we are being productive, which does not equal being effective. I believe when we set our priority straight we can get more done with less exertion or busyness.

There is nothing wrong with being busy when we are busy about the right things and sustaining our daily relationship with God. When we are busy about the things that God has told us to do we will be rewarded with strength and rest.

Thought Questions for Carrot of Busyness

Is it hard to settle down and just rest?

Am I busy and focusing my time on the most important things for my life, family, friends?

How do you feel when you are not busy?

Overcoming the Distraction (Carrot) of Impatience

Impatience, which is caused by anxiety, plays a significant role in distracting us from overcoming problems in our daily lives. When we become anxious for things we need or for things to happen in our lives, the carrot of impatience can easily begin to work as a major distraction. Anxiety and the need to have things "right now" can cause us to be impatient with others and also cause personal, mental, physical, and spiritual problems.

One thing should be clear from the start: God does not desire us to be impatient or to be anxious about anything! A familiar passage in the Bible that focuses on overcoming the distraction of impatience:

Philippians 4:6 *reads: Be anxious for nothing, but in everything, by prayer and supplication, with thanksgiving, let your requests be made known unto God. And the peace of God, which passes all understanding, shall guide your hearts and minds through Christ Jesus.*

However, there are so many daily examples of how anxiety and impatience will negatively influence our daily lives and distract us from overcoming in our daily lives. Here is a personal example: I am trying to get somewhere in a hurry and time is of the essence, it usually has me on edge. When I am waiting for someone or something, it is not always the easiest thing for me to do. I get restless sometimes, uneasy because I always have other responsibilities to address. This is especially true when there is nothing you can do but wait! How do you react? You may tend to jump ahead of waiting to try to make something happen. Not realizing that may lead to a shipwreck when one is impatient.

I can recall going to the nail shop to get my fingernails polished on a Friday afternoon after work. This seems like a relaxing thing to do after a stressful morning of working. The technician did an excellent job. I had to sit under a light for ten minutes for my nails to properly dry. The technician really expected me to sit for ten whole minutes and not move. Ten minutes sure seemed like a long time. As I began to sit and stare at the wall I noticed after about three minutes my foot started moving, after four minutes I started fidgeting around in my seat. Now it is five minutes, and I pulled my hands out from under the light and thought they looked dry. I lightly touched them, they also felt dry. I am ready to go, my nails are dry. I really did not need to wait ten WHOLE minutes. Well, I know you can guess what happened if you ever had your nails painted, you are right. When I opened the car door, I got a few dings. I ended up going back inside to ask the technician could she please touch up the dings in my nails that I messed up.

I had to start the process all over again. I had to ask myself do you have attention disorder or what? (Just saying). Ten minutes felt like a lifetime. I could not be patient enough just to wait for ten minutes. I had too much to do then to sit still for ten WHOLE minutes.

I emphasized the word **Ten Whole Minutes** because you and I know ten minutes is not a long time. I just had too much on my mind. I felt like I was wasting time just sitting. However, it was necessary that I waited the ten minutes so that my nails would be completely dry and sustainable in case they had to take a hit.

When you do not wait you can make unnecessary dings and bumps in life. We can avoid starting so many things all over again. I can hear my grandmother say if (you bump your head enough you will learn how to settle yourself down).

We can stay on the merry go round of life for a long time if we do not learn from our mistakes by not having patience. Wait and let the process work and we will get the benefit of not repeating the same mistakes over and over again. We will not get on people's nerves. Stop draining the people we love by having them to keep listening to us doing the same thing repeatedly. This can become exhausting on the listener's end. (Just saying)

With patience, we also will not miss the delicate details when we take our time and read the small print. You and I know by now it is in the small print that really is the most valuable information we need to be informed. But who has time to read the small print that we almost need a magnifying glass to read it? We all need to take out the time, so we know what we are about to commit to. It is easy to get into a contract or relationship and yet it is complicated to get released from it sometimes. Let us learn not to feel pressure to move too fast or answer a question too quickly.

One more example of being impatient: I notice how easy it is to commit to a relationship, phone service, security alarm system service or any kind of service with a contract. The frustration comes when you want to cancel or decline or disconnect a service or get out of a contract. You find out It is not anything like how you enter the service or relationship. You get the run around for instance: you want to disconnect from a service, so you make a phone call, and you are on hold listening to music played for five minutes.

Finally, you get to talk to a live person on the other end of the phone, you cannot see them, and all you are trying to do is cancel your service at the end of the contract and they ask you ten questions why you want to disconnect, and how can we keep you as a loyal customer.

You explain to them after a ten-minute conversation, and they preceded by offering you a lower rate or price. You are looking at the phone, and you so kindly respond mam, I just want to cancel my service, she responds like she did not hear anything that you said about canceling the service. Now your voice starts changing into a more upper registry. Once she hears your voice changing that is when she says, hold let me get you to our cancelation department. You are now on hold for another three minutes listening to the same annoying music. While waiting you start walking the floor and breathing a little faster because all you want to do is cancel your service. The cancellation department is now online asking you the same questions all over again. Once the cancelation department understand they cannot change your mind because your voice just changed from a high registry to now a low baritone, she has the nerve to say hold on I must get you to the cancelation specialist. They are the ones that will do the actual closing, now you are looking at your phone ready to hang it up because of the process you must go through. Finally, it is closed out!!! "SORRY, I'M JUST BEING A LITTLE TRANSPARENT!"

Well, in life it can get that intense, yet you must hang in there and go through the steps to the finish line. Unfortunately, we cannot skip some steps in life and still be able to grow properly. When we have patience to wait and complete the process, that is when we can get Final Closure in Our Situations the right way.

I am Thankful that our God is a Patient God Romans 15:5: (Now the God of patience and consolation grant you to be likeminded one toward another according to Christ Jesus). I am so glad God has patience with us, we would not have made it this far without him staying the course with us.

When it comes to relationships, every situation is different. God may want you to take your time before severance the commitment. The Lord may want to work something out of the relationship so he can work on some critical things that are needed to develop the relationship.

*It will take patience to keep the relationship intact before giving up on the commitment. You will see the reward of patience eventually when your union has been God ordained, it just needed to be refined. Isaiah 40:31 They that wait upon the Lord SHALL renew their strength; they SHALL mount up with wings as eagles; they SHALL run, and not get weary; and they SHALL walk, and not faint. You will mount up above your circumstances even if they do not change **You Will.***

*Keep walking and running, in other words keep moving, do not faint, you will be the one changing into a stronger and wiser individual because of learning to be an **Overcomer of the Carrot of Impatience**. Psalms 27:14 Wait on the Lord; Be of good courage, And he shall strengthen your heart; Wait, I say, on the Lord.*

*<u>**Lesson learned**</u>: waiting when needed is never wasting time. Wonderful things come out of having patience. The Bible states: Luke 21: 19 (In your patience you possess your souls); Going through the process in a hurry cost the technician extra time to do something all over again because I could not wait.*

Thought Questions for the Carrot of Impatience

Are you a Patient or Impatient Person?

What are some things I can <u>avoid</u> to be more Patient?

What are some things I can <u>do</u> to be more Patient?

Can you identify your triggers?

Overcoming The Distraction (Carrot) of Noise

I can hear the train whisking by so fast, the sound is so loud I cannot hear anything else until the rushing train passes by. The big train was as though it was coming right through the house. The glass in the curio cabinet is shaking and the vibration sometimes is unsettling when I want to rest. I go for a walk, and I hear the dogs barking as though they are having a conversation of their own. I am glad I cannot interpret what is being said in dog barking language. Birds are chirping, people are out walking and talking on the cell phone.

I enter the house and the washing machine is making its own kind of noise and the sound of running water seems endless. Then there comes the thumping, then the spinning before the calm. Phone calls to make, clicking of pots and pans for dinner.

*Surrounded by so much noise day by day minute by minute can begin to take over the ability to focus on quietness. One may even find themselves talking loud to the extent people may wonder why you are talking so loud when not needed. I went to a restaurant to have a nice romantic dinner and the music was so loud we ended up screaming at each other to have a conversation. Needless to say, we ate quickly and departed. This is a manifestation of the **Carrot of Noise!!!***

We must find the time to calm or quiet our Spirit, Mind, and our Body, so we can allow the peace of God to rule and work in our hearts.. This will also allow us to take time to look introspectively into our heart and mind, examining ourselves to see if we are on the correct path. We must find and take the time to ask ourselves: How am I doing? Am I focused on the right things? Am I listening to Gods voice and God's leading?

I was given a gift to get a massage for my birthday. While lying on the table with dim lighting, a wonderful back rub with calming relaxing music that just made you let your shoulders down. Yet the massage therapist repeatedly kept telling me to relax and let my shoulders drop.

It was at that point I realized I had become so intense in my day-to-day affairs. It brought tears to my eyes that I had become a stranger to quietness and calmness. It was as though we had drifted in two different directions. If this speaks to you today it is urgent that we must fight to find quietness in our lives.

Why is this so important? Thanks for asking: The book of Job, 33:31 in the Bible: Job was reminded of the Lord, Pay attention, Job, and listen to me. Be quiet, and I will speak. Vs: 33; Again, the Lord reminded him to be quiet, and I will teach you wisdom. Quietness is attached to our relationship with the Lord. That is our one-on-one time to be taught by the greatest teachers of all times.

Noise can become such a distraction especially when it gets into your head and you are not the one even talking, it is all the noise you heard from the day. We live in an age where there is so much chatter going on which can distract us from hearing the voice of the Lord. Wisdom comes from asking and being quiet. James 1:5 states now if any of you lacks wisdom, he should ask God-who gives to all generously and ungrudgingly—and it will be given to him.

Let us run back into the arms of quietness. While writing it is coming from a place of quietness. Right now, I am loving this sound of quietness, it is so calming and peaceful. I have entered a place that I once was familiar with and today we are reunited, and I can honestly say I have missed you. I hear you again speaking so tenderly and gently. This moment is taking my breath away to feel so connected to the one who speaks **Peace be Still**.

When the storm of life comes to conquer my soul there is yet a still quite voice that speaks so much louder until you do not feel the impact of the storm. Sometimes all you need is a word from the Lord, and you will sense the strength and the calmness from his voice. Blessed assurance Jesus is right here with us. Emmanuel {God with us}.

Try practicing sitting still for some time and just be quiet. It may feel awkward at first but the more you practice it, you will begin to see the benefit of stillness and quietness. **Overcoming the Carrot of noise** *that is trying to bombard our life. This is the goal going forward.*

Overcoming the Distraction (Carrot) of No Accountability

I know we all would like to make the best decisions for our life when it comes to family, finances, friends, careers, relationships, and many other major activities in which we are involved. When it comes to decisions that affect us for good or for bad, it helps to have someone to bounce things off of or someone who can simply hear us out, to help confirm the correctness (or lack thereof), of our thoughts and ideas. This will help bring clarity and provide better decisions.

When we decide on a person to hear us out and to help confirm our thoughts and ideas, this should be a person we have confidence in; someone we can trust, who has the knowledge, expertise or wisdom and experience in the area or topic we are dealing with. The person may be an elderly person with extraordinarily little education; however, they may have much wisdom and experience under their belt. Experience along with head knowledge can go a long way when needing a little assistance in making some major decisions.

*The **Carrot of No Accountability** is when we are not accountable for the actions we take or the ideas we promote. When a person checks with someone other than themself, it is like having an extra set of eyes and ears connected to ours.' However, when we DON'T check with someone else, someone we can trust to validate our thoughts and ideas, we may be putting ourself in a position where we DO NOT recognize that there are other ways to address our problem. <u>An accountability partner can provide a unique perspective or confirm the thoughts we already have on a situation.</u>*

If we are a person that always makes our own decisions, without counsel from others, we can easily lead ourself off track and be distracted by the outcome of our own decisions. Many bad relationships, poor financial decisions, wrong career choices, etc., are made when people fail to consult with anyone to get another perspective. It can only benefit us when we listen to another trusted person's perspective before making any major decision. We may not agree with their input, but it still provides some balanced input before we make a major decision.

There is no harm in talking to a trusted person that has our best interest in mind. Even if their input goes against our decision. This shows that we are wise and humble enough to consider a difference of opinion without shutting anyone else's advice down after all, (we do not know everything) oh, I am sorry I just hurt someone feelings right there.

Many people have already made up their mind what they are planning to do, with no plans to consult with anyone else. They make their decision and have no accountability to anyone, which in many cases leaves out major considerations in their decision making. A wrong decision can have an impact on you for months, years and yes, even a lifetime. An accountability partner can be a blessing, by providing the needed information to make good balanced decisions. An accountability partner should be someone we know and trust, to help us make sound decisions and to make sure we are seeing all there is to see in our situation.

Today's world is a place where people easily lose trust in others. People are very quick to "lean on their own understanding, and not be accountable for their own decisions." I have learned that sometimes depending on the place that we are at in life emotionally and mentally, can shape and alter your decision making. Trials and tests will come into our lives and may distract us from making the best decision.

Therefore, it is imperative to be accountable to someone that we consider an accountability partner to bring balance to the decisions we make. <u>Proverbs 11:14</u> states: "Where no counsel is, the people fall: but in the multitude of counsellors there is safety." Let us make safe decisions. Most of all seek wisdom from the Lord and be intentional on submitting one to another so we can truly be an **Overcomer of the Carrot of No Accountability.**

Questions for Carrot of No Accountability

Do you have an accountability partner?

If not, why?

How do you handle Constructive Criticism?

Notes

When I examine myself, my behavior, my relationships, my words, what do I see (good, bad, changes)?

Overcoming the Distraction (Carrot) of False News

There is a new type of news that has invaded our country and the world at large. It is called "False News." Some of the news networks have been tagged as providing "False News." This is due to the fact that they tell part of the story or because they tell the news with their "spin" on the story. These News providers take their "editorial privilege" and tell the news in a way that spins the truth in favor of their own political or organization bias. This approach has been the cause for much of the political divide, racial divide, economic divide, and many other divisive positions in our world today.

One of the biblical principles that I learned early in life is this. "A half lie is still a lie. A three quarters (3/4) lie is still a lie." Therefore, a 90% true story is still not Truth, and 95% news story is still "False News." Editorial privilege may be okay for the Broadcasting networks, but it is a partial truth with an editorial spin and is still "False News." It makes no difference which News Broadcasting network provides the news, if part of the story is left out, or part of the story is assumed to be the case: it is still a LIE and NOT TRUE and is considered False news! If you are only telling part of the story and not all of it, or aggerating a point that is still considered false news.

Living in this natural world today, with social media, worldwide broadcasting, and instant electronic communications, fake and erroneous news is a daily experience and distraction. Many of these distractions serve as entertainment to capture our thoughts on unproductive and foolish ideas. People are easily entertained by anything that comes across the news reel. Anyone can easily observe people today, who hold their electronic devices in their hands and constantly stroll through the messages on their devices to see or become aware of something new. Much of the latest information we read or see on our devices is partial information, part of the story.

However, part of the story is still worth publishing by the networks because it is something new to talk about (<u>Acts 17:21 people's talk about something NEW</u>). The gap in the news always leaves room for interpretation, half-truths, lies and miscommunication, which lead to FALSE NEWS.

We must be careful and, on our guard, not to confuse half or partial news with TRUTH. **Yes, even what we consider to be our truth still may not be the truth.** *For instance: you could look in the mirror and think to yourself I am so ugly, that is not true, that is the way you are feeling mentally, but the truth is you are fearfully and wonderfully made Psalms 139: 14, that is the TRUTH. There is really only one source of truth, which has been proven down through the ages. The Bible, though controversial with many religions, etc., has still stood the test of time, and for over 4,000 years and counting, has been the source of TRUTH, with foundational principles that still hold this world together up to this current moment.*

There is nothing false or half true about the what Jesus and other Biblical figures have said. The foundations of God's Word are sure. (2nd Timothy 2:19). Through the Word of God, we are able to discern what is false news and what is truth. False news is remarkably similar to what we consider today as a "knock off brand." This is a brand of clothing or other materials that look remarkably similar to the real thing but is a counterfeit or fake representation of the real thing. It is hard for some to distinguish the difference. However, a seeker of the genuine brand will make sure they are purchasing the real thing and not a counterfeit, knock off or fake item. False news comes across in the same way: it sounds fresh, it is updated news, with some facts that are true, so it must be right or relevant! Correct? Absolutely NOT. Real truth will stand the test of time, when all the facts are revealed, and the real thing is tried and tested to be truth. We know the truth when we see the evidence and the outcome.

This is why we believe the truth of the Bible. Jesus said what he came here to do. He did it: all we have to do is believe it. His Good News is Great News and not False News.

So many things in life have value such as gold, fine linen, and currency, yet nothing is as priceless as the truth. John 8:32 states and you still know the truth, and the truth shall make you free. At the end of the misinformation that is in our world at large today is misleading, when there is no real content or value.

The Bible says the devil is the Father of Lies and he will fool the very elect if were possible. Listen, we must know what is true and what is false. This is just another distraction to get us off track.

If you find yourself drifting away from what are the most important things in life due to false information and misinformation you must guard the truth and not let other myths creep in. False doctrines, myths, misinterpretations are heavily on the rise and confusing our nation at large. We see on the rise mental health being challenged like never before. This could be the work of believing everything you hear and see that does not line up with The Truth.

Living in such a fake and counterfeit age, many people are not satisfied with how God designed them and how they actually look. The enemy has crept in to make people feel like they need to help God out when he put them together the way he uniquely made you. You can begin to change and add on and take away or should I say cut away until they have become unrecognizable. You used to like yourself now you find yourself needing to look and be somebody God never intended you to be.

We all have a responsibility to what we listen to and what we read and watch on television. We must guard what we allow to go into our minds. Once you continue listening to incorrect information continuously it will begin to impact your thoughts. So, stop it right now, so you can have a sound mind and not be manipulated into thinking the wrong way due to false news.

Let us stay true to God, ourselves, to others and be the peculiar people God called us to be. Truth is always clear, no fantasy, no myths, and no false news. The outcome of truth will lead you on the right path of righteousness to do the right thing.

*Truth always lines up with the Word of God. The best news in the world is the gospel. The gospel is good news and glad tidings. Living in times like these with so much depressing news and false news coming at us all the time It is so refreshing to read and hear something that encourages, uplifts, and gives us hope to overcome so many of these distractions. The gospel is what gives us the strength to be **Overcomers against the false news** and embrace Gods truth for he is TRUTH. Gods word is profitable for our day-to-day life. The news of the gospel spread across the world, and the message bought hope to all who received the truth. (Jesus Saves)!!!!*

Questions for carrot of False News

1. **What can we do to protect ourselves from false news that promotes negative thoughts, divisive ideas, and harmful images?**

2. **How can we apply this scripture to our lives to Overcome false news? (Philippians 4:8)**

Overcoming the Distractions (Carrot) of Gifts and Talents

God has shown His grace and favor to the human race by giving us all various gifts and talents. The Book of James, in the New Testament, chapter one, verse seventeen lets us know that "Every good and perfect gift comes from our great God who is above." The primary reason our God given gifts can become distractions is the fact that we so often take ownership of these gifts as if our efforts actually generated the gift or talent. When we begin to use our gifts and talents, given to us by God our creator, and we flaunt or boast about our efforts and our accomplishments as if they have been self-generated, we disconnect with the source from whom all blessings and gifts come from. We then begin to talk and operate as if our gifts and talents have been birthed and cultivated solely by our own efforts. Many people, at this stage engage in marketing their God given gifts as their own original creation, their brand, their efforts; not realizing the fact that we have drifted off course, forgetting to give God all the Glory for the wonderful gifts and talents He has given us!

One of the key causes of being distracted by our God given gifts and talents is when we FAIL to recognize where all good and perfect gifts, talents and abilities come from. However, we must remember the fact that just because we have a gift, it may not always be used in the ways GOD INTENDED! Satan is the unseen deceiver here on earth. Satan, in many ways and countless times, deceives people into using their gifts and talents to influence people in the wrong way and for the wrong reasons. THE BIBLE SAYS: (KJV James 1:17) **_EVERY GOOD AND PERFECT GIFT_** **_COMES FROM ABOVE_**. *Our gifts and talent have been given to us to do good and not evil or to lead people astray. Our gifts and talents have also been given to bring glory to God alone, not to ourselves.*

It is imperative for us to realize this fact so that we do not deceive people by glorifying ourselves as someone or something great. Self-exaltation (WHICH IS REALLY SELF DECEPTION), is clearly not from above. If we use our gifts for the wrong reasons, it will lift us up, but self-exaltation is never good and perfect. When we allow a gift or a talent to become something that we take credit for and we exalt ourselves, taking the honor for something only God can give, we open ourselves up to be distracted by the enemy of our soul.

This can cause a gift or talent to become an idol in our lives; one that we worship or even self-worship. The goal of the distraction is to cause us to take our eyes off of our gracious God and to place our focus on ourselves. We must guard and protect ourselves from this type of distraction. For we live in a world that acknowledges and rewards people for their gifts and talents continuously. In the United States alone, we will recognize and award people for their gifts, talents, accomplishments. Every year we hear of the: Emmy Award winners, Sports Awards winners, Veterans awards, Oscar Awards, BET awards, Stella awards, Grammy Awards, and on and on. There is nothing wrong with honoring people for their efforts, where it is due. However, when it comes to recognizing where All of these gifts and talents come from, Most people fail to recognize God Almighty, the giver of every GOOD AND PERFECT gift that we possess. Awards and recognition that we give to ourselves are not bad in and of themselves. However, If we fail to recognize our Almighty God in everything we do, the negative spirit will enter in and, DANGLE THE CARROT of Gifts and Talents" before us and will quickly label us as the source of our gift and/or talent. People love recognition. Once again, there is nothing wrong with acknowledging people for their efforts and work. However, we must learn the importance of acknowledging God in everything we do.

We live in a time when the demands for performance challenge us daily. We must guard against distractions that our gifts and talents may bring to us based on our performance.

We are often rewarded based on our performance. At our workplaces and in many extracurricular activities which, we can easily be distracted and not focus on what is most important.

You may just want to be a mom or dad that enjoys the simplicity of life such as: taking your children for a walk in the park. However, you no longer can find the time to do this because of the demands to use your gift or talent, which takes away from family time. Another example, you may want to have a romantic night with your spouse out alone with no interruptions.

How about just simply being you without any expectations or having a plastered smile that you learned how to wear even if it was not from the heart. Is it possible you can learn how to perform and wear a mask even while dealing with depression or suicidal thoughts? People can be more in love with your gift than you the person.

God gave you that gift or talent for a specific purpose. Your gift will make room for you and bring you before great men (PROVERBS 18:16). You never know where your talent or gift may show up in your life. It may or may not be on a platform with thousands of people. It may be in a supermarket, parking lot, your place of employment or with your family. So, it is imperative that we watch over our gifts and talents, and make sure we use them for the glory of God and not for ourselves.

I am reminded of a scripture in the bible Romans 1:25 states; (Who change the truth of God into a lie and worshipped and served the creature more than the Creator. We must recognize our gifts and talents that come from our Creator to bring him glory and to help others. Unfortunately, mankind always has another agenda to exploit and make money off any Gift and talent for their greed.

This is such a distraction when you are constantly being pulled to show up with your A game all the time. That is a lot of pressure which is taking folks out of here early. You may want to reflect on how much do people really care about you the person.

This happens all the time with Entertainers, Preachers, Businesspeople, Politicians, Authors, and Athletes. If there's money to be made off your gift or talent, the sharks are waiting to pimp the GIFT God gave you to bless the world to help, bring souls to him. You must realize it is not your gift to be misused.

In the Bible there is a story about a man name Samson who had a gift of strength from God (Judges Chapters 13-16). He was a physically strong and confident man who trusted in God for his strength. He had Gods favor on his life until he got around someone who took advantage of his gift for money. The problem was he shared the source of his strength with someone who was not interested in his source (God Almighty) but was solely interested in their own personal wellbeing. Samson did not realize at first the impact that bad relationships with people who do not share your beliefs can have on your gift or talents. Once he shared his personal source of his strength with a deceiving person who did not share his beliefs, she cut of his source of strength and gifting from God. His strength and his connection to his source were both gone once he connected with the wrong person. He did not realize he had lost the gift of strength that God had blessed him with until it was too late, and his enemies captured him and bound him with chains in prison for the rest of his life. Samson's story is a good example of the importance of protecting the gifts and talents that God has given to each of us. We must protect the gifts and talents that God has bless us with and make sure we are guarding our relationships against those who will harm us and mean us no good.

One last point on Samson: When he lost his gift and the source of his strength, he continued to try to exercise his gift, just as he did before. He quickly learned that being cut off from the source of his strength, he could go through the motions, but without God, his gift was not effective. He tried to do like he did previously, but without God, the source of his gift, the source of his strength, he could do nothing against his enemies. Question: Could that be you, like Samson, trying to use the gift or gifts that God gave you, while your relationship with God has been cut off or is non-existent? As with Samson, when there is no relationship with God, there is no connection with the source of all gifts and talents, there is no power, no anointing behind your actions or activity.

To enable your God given gifts and talents to be effective, you must have a relationship with God Almighty, the one who gives and graces us with All gifts and Talents. You may still be able to stir up emotions and do some things like you did before. However, your relationship with the Almighty God is what is needed to make a lasting impact to others here on this planet. When Samson finally reconnected with his source, he was able to take down all of his enemies in one final event in his life, which had a life ending impact on the entire Kingdom of the Philistines (Judges Chap 16). Let us stay true to God, ourselves, to others and be the peculiar people God called us to be.

Gifts and Talents are a natural part of all of our lives. The important point in all of this is the fact that we must recognize where our gifts and talents come from (God Almighty): And as we recognize this and use our gifts accordingly (Giving God all the Glory for his great and precious gifts and talents), we will gain strength and have peace with God, while being a blessing to everyone else.

To Overcome the distraction (carrots) of gifts and talents, *one must remain humble and have a heart of gratitude. Remember to always keep a standard and not compromise with the world's way of doing things. Strive to become a gift to other people so you can help make this world a better place to live in. Always remember Gods reward will always overcome what people can offer. What People offer is usually limited but our God offers, can and will do the impossible.*

Questions for the Carrot of Gifts and Talents

Do you believe you have a gift or talent?

What comes natural to you that brings you joy?

Are you still in discovery mode of what God has place in you?

What has God gifted you with and how can you use your gift to bless others?

Overcoming the Distraction (Carrot) of Miscommunication

Wholesome and healthy communication is always good, but it is not always easy to accomplish. Often, we have conversations with the intent to encourage and build up. However, the wrong words can quickly move you away from having good and productive conversations. In addition, often times while communicating with others, we fail to listen intently and acknowledge what the person we are communicating with is dealing with at the time. We must learn the importance of being considerate and understanding of what people are dealing with and what people are going through at that time before we engage in conversation. You also must develop the discipline of avoiding certain behaviors for your conversations to be productive. Such as: You are having a conversation; one person just wants to respond without really listening to understand what the other person is trying to say: Or one person has their guard up while the other person is being dismissive to whatever the other person is trying to communicate. Have you ever walked away from a conversation and said to yourself: "Did they even hear anything I said?." This is where the seeds of miscommunication are sown, and it can become a major distraction in relationships.

Listening is key in order to have effective communication. Good listening skills will enable us to have a clear understanding of how we should respond or react to the person we are communicating with. While authoring this book, I acknowledge the fact that I still had a lot of work to do in this area of listening while communicating. I was having a conversation recently and I blew it by not listening first to the person I was communicating with. He was a young man who was a customer service representative waiting on me. He began sharing with me about a problematic situation he was going through. Before long, I had interjected my story into the conversation. I did not allow him to finish his story that he had been explaining to me.

Before I recognized it, the person never had an opportunity to share his entire story with me, I am sure he walked away feeling like he was not heard. This was a distraction of miscommunication. Even though we had a friendly conversation, I was not able to help him because I failed to listen to his actual problem: the **carrot of miscommunication**.

I am thankful for the fact that I have grown enough now to recognize how I can communicate better, learning to listen first when someone comes to me. This is a skill that takes time and work. It can be more difficult to listen especially when it seems like people come to you often for advice. The communication skill of listening more to another person's story without me sharing my own similar story, was a lesson for me to learn. It is essential if we are to be a good communicator and do not want to distract others from coming to us for help and guidance. In this particular case, the young man stopped talking from sharing his story and was forced to listen to my story. He walked away distracted with no real solution to his problem. He really needed someone to listen to him(wow.)

When I got in my vehicle, I felt bad, and I thought that was an opportunity for this young man to share his story. My position should have been for me to show empathy for his situation and not for me to be insensitive to what he was going through. Even though our stories were similar I still needed to hold my story for another time. Sometimes we need to really think before speaking and discern which way we are to communicate by listening or by speaking. Hearing is an action word; (to give ear to). My prayer is that we will have **the Power to hear when listening**. *I believe our paths will cross again because I shop at the store (that the young man works at) every now in then. Hopefully, I will get it right when I talk to him the next time.*

This lesson on miscommunication and listening is important in all of our relationships. It is important that our spouse, our children, and our friends know how critical listening is. We do not want to miss the opportunity to communicate clearly. This is also how we build strong relationships when we can improve our listening and other communication skills.

If we are not willing to communicate by listening with the intent to understand the other person, we may miss some valuable interaction with the party with which we are communicating. It may take a little time, but some may be worth the work that we put in. Once we work at communicating it may begin to flow better with people that seem like you are from two different plants.

In communicating we can never win an argument by talking at each other and not to each other. Arguing leads nowhere when wanting to communicate in a constructive manner. We must remember, the challenge could come from our environment, the way we were raised or our education so many factors play apart how we communicate. The fact of the matter is as long as we live among people we must communicate; the question is how will you?

In close relationships it is important that we take the time to be intentional on connecting in communicating with respect and empathy if needed. When communicating with the intent to understand the heart of what the person is expressing, it is so much more important than just hearing what they are saying.

Let us overcome this **Distraction of Miscommunication** *by being intentional on Listening first as well as talking to get a full understanding. It is beneficial to learn this combined art of connecting in conversations.*

A valuable tool to use is connecting words such as: in addition to what you are saying, I hear what you are saying, I respect what you are saying, or can you explain what you are saying a little better I would appreciate.

It is important to respect what others are saying when you want to have a healthy wholesome conversation and effective communication. Yes, even when we must have some hard or tough conversations when necessary. We must confront these types of conversations when the time is right time, in order to keep our heart pure with the other person, and not be afraid to express what it is that we really want to say. For some people, we have just learned how to keep swallowing our emotions and concerns for the sake of keeping peace. That was one of my mother's favorite sayings (Just be quiet to keep the peace); in other words, disregard how you feel and what you think, avoiding any confrontation. However, at times confrontation is needed to fully communicate.

(WOW) What I found out is if you do not express yourself, thoughts, and concerns, fully communicating, eventually you will regurgitate every emotion and thought, and it will be nasty when it comes out, making the problem worse.

Some other aspects of miscommunicating are caused when we talk without connecting with the person or having eye-to-eye contact. Social media and texting have become a major source of this type of communication and one of the current ways of personally talking with each other. We must learn to pick up the phone and call, facetime call, meet in person. The world's advancements in technology should not cause us to become more socially awkward in not knowing how to talk face to face, and truly communicate with each other. We should truly meet and communicate with one another, eye to eye, face to face, learning to connect with one another by talking and fellowshipping with one another.

Communicating verbally, face to face, is the best way to build strong relationships, while reducing or eliminating the poor or miscommunication can hinder or destroy good relationships. Let us work on being a builder of communication for strong relationships. I am finding out the power in communicating Gods way can bring life to someone in need of encouragement or a word of rebuke that would save a life.

Summary

Carrots of distractions dangle before us, some are pleasing to the eye, and some are great opportunities. This attraction is what makes us want to chase after the many distractions of life. As long as we are alive there will be something or someone that will try to interfere or distract us from our purpose along life's path. Distractions have a way of knocking at your door, even when you think you are a focused person. We must remember, to overcome life's distractions, we need to stay focused on God's directions (the Bible) and renew our thoughts every day in prayer and dependency on God's grace. His Grace is sufficient to meet our needs, every day!

To Overcome the Distractions of Life *each day: We must Set boundaries, We must Stick to our word and be smart about our choices. We must anticipate the unseen distractions and use discernment in all our decisions, based on the Word of God: We must also have an accountability partner or someone that is God centered that we have confidence in, that we can share our hearts and thoughts with to help us in our time of need.*

A useful tool to use is keeping a daily log of the things that you want to be a priority each day. Identify triggers that get you off track and cause you to be unfocused. Take time to rest and find a quiet place to renew, regroup, refill, and refocus for the next day (day by day).

Another good practice to learn is how to encourage yourself every morning with a song, or words of affirmation, along with prayer and fellowship with God.

This book is intended for young adults, middle-aged adults, and senior adults.

Round Table Discussions

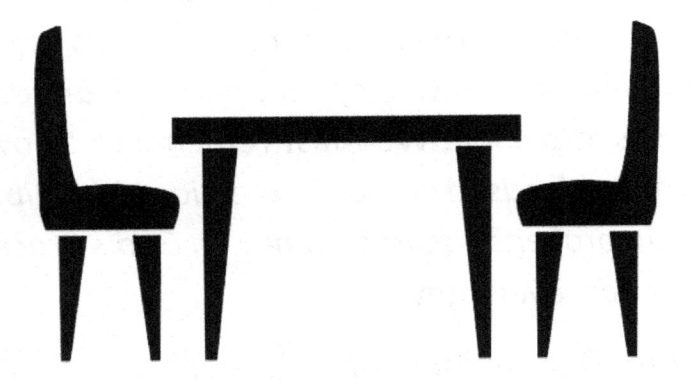

Words of Encouragement

This book is designed for those who are willing to trust God and do the work that is necessary to overcome the many distractions that come into our lives. You can be assured, distractions will come. It is critically important that we train our minds to stay focused, no matter what trial, temptation, wrong connection, failure, or success that comes into our lives. 1 John 4;4 says, Ye are of God, little children, and have overcome them: because greater is he that is in you, than he that is in the world. Let us walk as overcomers, pacing ourselves and being watchful of distractions. This way we will be walking in purpose, on purpose, with God's guidance.

***Crystal Pippins**, together with her husband, Henry Pippins, are the founders of Total Life Center, NFP, a Non-Profit-Training Organization. Crystal is the original designer and director of the Total Life Training physical fitness program. She developed the original fitness routines and exercise plans when the organization started back in 2002. Her 22 plus years of service, leadership and inspiration for the <u>Total Life Training, Non-Profit Organization</u> has been the constant force that has kept this organization expanding into the four different states, in which the Pippins have lived over the past 22 years. Crystal continues to lead this organization as her and her husband have most recently relocated to the Atlanta, Georgia metro-area. Crystal, most recently authored the 2018 book, entitled "<u>When Life Dangles You a Carrot</u>." This book was the foundational truth that led to this current publication, "<u>Overcoming the Distractions (Carrots) of Life.</u>" Crystal is the mother of three children, Caretaker to one of her siblings, Grandmother to twelve and great grandmother to nine. Crystal R. Pippins committed her life to Jesus Christ over 44 years ago and has been involved in Christian Ministry for almost 40 years. Crystal Pippins is the wife of the Reverend Dr. Henry J. Pippins Jr. for 33 years. She has served as Co-Pastor and Associate Minister in Christian Churches in Pennsylvania, New York, Seattle, WA, Chicago/Joliet, IL, St. Augustine, FL, and Indianapolis, IN. As one of the founders of <u>Total Life Training NPO</u>, Now presently living in Douglasville GA. Crystal has been involved and effective in most all aspects of Life Skills Training and Christian Counseling. Christian Education certificate from Tabernacle University (Goldsboro, N.C.), Hudson Valley College, (NY), Medical Assistant Diploma from Antonelli Medical School, (PA).) She is a life-long Learner and Teacher. Crystal develops workshops, empowerment conferences and provides resources for council to those who are in physical and spiritual need. Crystal's heart and passion is to help people, especially those who need help in gaining a full and true knowledge of the Lord Jesus Christ: This is the catalyst behind her writing this sequel book, Overcoming Distractions (Carrots) of Life.*

Highlights

1. *Start your day off with prayer/meditation*

2. *Look intently at yourself and no one else*

3. *Be Honest with yourself*

4. *Address the wrong choices*

5. *Attack pride, shame, and quilt*

6. *Let go of past failures*

7. *Have an accountability partner*

8. *Communicate to understand*

9. *Have a readiness to address distractions that come to get us off track.*

10. *Ask God for his wisdom and do not lean to your own understanding*

Your Challenge

What will you take away and put into practice to improve your life from reading Overcoming the Distractions (carrots) of Life?

To Purchase Copies

Amazon.com

Email: pippins@totallifetraining.com

Website: Totallifetraining.com

Overcoming The Distractions (Carrots) of Life

May you be Blessed and Walk in God's Grace that is sufficient for you today!

Crystal R. Pippins

Made in the USA
Columbia, SC
02 August 2024